C++ Programming

From Novice to Expert in a Step-by-Step
Journey

Ryan Campbell

Contents

Contents

Introduction

Are you ready to embark on an exhilarating journey into the world of programming, where creativity knows no bounds, and innovation becomes second nature? Look no further! Welcome to the immersive realm of C++, a programming language that has been hailed as the gateway to endless possibilities in the digital universe.

In this comprehensive guide, we'll take you by the hand and lead you through the mesmerizing landscapes of C++. Whether you're a complete novice or an aspiring coder looking to elevate your skills, this book is tailor-made to suit your needs.

Why C++? The Power of Possibilities

C++ isn't just any programming language; it's an empowering tool that grants you the freedom to breathe life into your ideas. Picture yourself crafting intricate applications, building robust software, or even exploring the enchanting realm of game development. With C++, the power to shape your dreams into reality rests at your fingertips.

A Journey Paved with Knowledge

Every great adventure starts with a solid foundation, and that's precisely what we'll provide you with in this book. We begin with an enchanting introduction to C++, where you'll discover its significance and rich history, leaving you eager to embrace the exciting world of coding.

Embark on a Learning Odyssey

We believe that learning should be an invigorating voyage, not a tedious task. That's why we've carefully designed this guide to be your trusty companion, guiding you through each step with clarity and enthusiasm. Unravel the mystery of data types and variables, delve into control structures and decision-making processes, and wield the power of functions and modular programming to create elegant and efficient code.

Venture into Advanced Realms

As your expertise blossoms, so will the complexity of your projects. Fear not, intrepid explorer! We'll equip you with the knowledge of pointers and memory management, allowing you to wield memory like a seasoned wizard. Dive into the enchanting world of object-oriented programming, where you'll master the art of crafting elegant and scalable applications that leave a lasting impact.

Unlock the Gates of Creativity

C++ isn't just a tool; it's a magical wand that can breathe life into your wildest ideas. We'll equip you with advanced concepts, such as templates and exception handling, that will empower you to push the boundaries of what's possible. Together, we'll unleash the full potential of C++, allowing your creativity to soar to new heights.

The Gateway to Real-World Impact

What good is knowledge without application? Prepare to be amazed as we showcase real-world applications of C++ in diverse domains. From financial applications to cutting-edge technology, you'll witness the transformational impact of your newfound skills in the tangible world around you.

Your Adventure Awaits!

So, are you ready to embark on this thrilling odyssey into the heart of C++ programming? Whether you're a curious beginner or an aspiring coding virtuoso, this book is your key to unlock a world of endless opportunities. Step into the realm of C++, and let the magic of programming ignite your passion and lead you towards an extraordinary future.

Are you prepared to unleash your programming potential? If the answer is a resounding "YES," then let's begin your adventure now! The captivating world of C++ awaits your arrival.

Chapter 1: Understanding Data Types and Variables

The Building Blocks

In the realm of computer programming, understanding data types and variables is akin to mastering the language's grammar and vocabulary. They form the very foundation upon which all code is constructed and manipulated. In this chapter, we shall delve into the fundamental concepts of data types and variables in the C++ programming language, equipping you with the essential building blocks needed to craft elegant and efficient code.

The Essence of Data in Programming

Before we immerse ourselves in the intricacies of data types and variables, let us first grasp the significance of data in the realm of programming.

At its core, computer programming is the art of instructing machines to perform specific tasks. These tasks, in turn, involve the manipulation and processing of data. Data can take various forms, ranging from simple integers and characters to complex structures and objects.

Data comes in many flavors, each suited for specific purposes. Therefore, it is crucial for a programmer to understand the characteristics of different data types and the ways they interact with the underlying hardware. This understanding will enable us to optimize code execution, conserve memory, and ensure the reliability of our programs.

The Building Blocks: Data Types

In C++, data types are the building blocks that define the nature of data and dictate the operations that can be performed on them. C++

offers a rich variety of data types, catering to diverse programming needs. Let us explore some of the primary data types that lay the groundwork for our coding endeavors:

Fundamental Data Types

1. **Integer Types (int)**: Representing whole numbers, integer types encompass various ranges of values, from small integers like -32768 to large ones like 32767. Understanding the range of integer types is vital for handling computations, avoiding overflows, and optimizing memory usage.

2. **Floating-Point Types (float, double)**: Dealing with real numbers, floating-point types offer a level of precision that accommodates decimal values. Programmers must be cautious about

floating-point precision errors, as they can affect the accuracy of calculations.

3. **Character Types (char)**: Responsible for representing single characters, character types allow the manipulation of individual characters and ASCII values, essential for handling text data.

4. **Boolean Type (bool)**: Booleans are binary data types, representing either true or false.

User-Defined Data Types

1. **Enumerations (enum)**: Enumerations enable the creation of custom data types with a set of named values, enhancing code readability and organization.

2. **Structures (struct)**: Structures enable the grouping of related variables under a single

user-defined data type, facilitating the handling of complex data structures.

3. **Classes (class)**: In the realm of object-oriented programming, classes provide the blueprint for creating objects with properties (variables) and behaviors (functions).

Variables: Containers of Data

Now that we have acquainted ourselves with data types, let us explore how they manifest in our programs through variables. In C++, variables act as containers that store data of specific data types in memory. Each variable is associated with a memory address, allowing us to access and manipulate the stored data.

Variable Declaration and Initialization

In C++, declaring a variable involves specifying its data type and an optional initial value. The declaration informs the compiler about the variable's existence and reserves memory for it. Initialization, on the other hand, assigns an initial value to the variable at the time of declaration.

```cpp
// Declaration and Initialization of Variables
int age;           // Declaration without initialization
int score = 100;   // Declaration with initialization
```

Variable Naming Rules

Naming variables follows certain rules in C++. Variable names must begin with a letter (uppercase or lowercase) or an underscore and can be followed by letters, digits, or underscores. They are case-sensitive, meaning that **myVar** and **myvar** would be considered distinct variables.

```
int myVariable;         // Valid variable name
double _temperature;    // Valid variable name
int 3numbers;           // Invalid variable name (starts with a digit)
```

Constants: Unchanging Data

In addition to variables, C++ allows the creation of constants, which are fixed values that do not change during program execution. Constants are declared using the **const** keyword and play a vital role in making code more robust and easier to maintain.

```
const int MAX_SCORE = 100; // Declaring a constant with the value 100
```

In this chapter, we have explored the essential building blocks of C++ programming: data types and variables. We have seen how data types define the nature of data and its behavior, while variables act as containers that store this data in memory. With a firm understanding of these concepts, you now possess the tools to begin crafting code that can perform powerful computations, manipulate data, and pave the way for more sophisticated programming endeavors.

In the next chapter, we shall venture further into the heart of C++, exploring control structures and decision-making processes, which will empower you to direct the flow of your programs with precision and finesse. So, let us continue this remarkable journey of mastering C++ and unlocking the true potential of computer programming.

Chapter 2: Control Structures and Decision Making

Directing Your Programs

In the world of computer programming, the ability to direct the flow of execution is a skill that separates novices from seasoned developers. Control structures and decision-making processes form the essence of this art, enabling programmers to create dynamic and responsive applications. In this chapter, we shall embark on an exploration of control structures, loops, and conditional statements in the C++ programming language. By understanding these powerful tools, you will gain control over your programs and unlock the potential to craft sophisticated and efficient solutions.

Controlling the Flow: Control Structures

At its core, a program is a sequence of instructions executed one after another. Control structures introduce a degree of flexibility, allowing us to alter the order of execution based on specific conditions or repetitions. In C++, we have three primary control structures: conditional statements, loops, and branching.

Conditional Statements

Conditional statements enable us to make decisions within our programs, directing the flow based on certain conditions. The most common conditional statement is the **if** statement, which executes a block of code only if a specified condition is true.

```
int age = 25;

if (age >= 18) {
    cout << "You are an adult." << endl;
} else {
    cout << "You are a minor." << endl;
}
```

The **if** statement can be extended with **else if** and **else** clauses to handle multiple conditions.

```
int score = 85;

if (score >= 90) {
    cout << "You got an A!" << endl;
} else if (score >= 80) {
    cout << "You got a B!" << endl;
} else {
    cout << "You got a C or lower." << endl;
}
```

Loops: Repeating the Process

Loops provide a mechanism to execute a block of code repeatedly until a specified condition is met.

In C++, we have three primary loop structures: **for**, **while**, and **do-while**.

The **for** Loop

The **for** loop is ideal when we know the number of iterations in advance.

```cpp
for (int i = 1; i <= 5; i++) {
    cout << i << " ";
}
```

The **while** Loop

```cpp
int i = 1;
while (i <= 5) {
    cout << i << " ";
    i++;
}
```

The **do-while** Loop

The **do-while** loop is similar to the **while** loop but guarantees the code block to execute at least once, even if the condition is false initially.

```cpp
int i = 1;
do {
    cout << i << " ";
    i++;
} while (i <= 5);
```

Branching: break and continue

In certain situations, we might need to break out of a loop prematurely or skip the current iteration and proceed to the next one. C++ provides the **break** and **continue** statements for these purposes.

```cpp
for (int i = 1; i <= 10; i++) {
    if (i == 5) {
        break;        // Exit the loop when i is 5
    }
    cout << i << " ";
}
```

```cpp
for (int i = 1; i <= 10; i++) {
    if (i % 2 == 0) {
        continue;   // Skip even numbers and proceed to the next iteration
    }
    cout << i << " ";
}
```

Making Informed Decisions: Conditional Operators

In addition to **if** statements, C++ offers conditional operators that allow for concise decision-making processes. These operators are frequently used when assigning values or evaluating expressions.

Ternary Operator

The ternary operator **?** **:** is a concise way to express a simple **if-else** statement.

23

```
int age = 20;
string result = (age >= 18) ? "Adult" : "Minor";
cout << "You are: " << result << endl;
```

Logical Operators

Logical operators, such as **&&** (AND), **||** (OR)

```
bool isRainy = true;
bool hasUmbrella = false;

if (isRainy && !hasUmbrella) {
    cout << "You might get wet!" << endl;
}
```

In this chapter, we have embarked on a thrilling journey through control structures and decision-making processes in C++ programming. We have explored the power of conditional statements, enabling us to make informed choices within our programs. Additionally, we have learned how to wield the might of loops, allowing us to repeat tasks efficiently. With the knowledge of branching, we can control the flow of execution in a more dynamic and flexible manner.

In the next chapter, we shall dive into the heart of C++ programming, where we will explore functions and modular programming. These concepts will empower you to create elegant and reusable code, unlocking the true potential of your programming prowess. So, let us continue this exhilarating adventure and elevate our programming skills to new heights.

Chapter 3: Functions and Modular Programming

Writing Efficient Code

In the realm of computer programming, the ability to create efficient and reusable code is an art form revered by seasoned developers. Functions and modular programming provide the key to unlock this mastery, enabling programmers to break down complex tasks into smaller, manageable pieces. In this chapter, we shall embark on a journey to learn the art of creating functions and organizing code into modules in the C++ programming language. By the end of this chapter, you will possess the skills to write elegant and efficient code that can be reused and maintained with ease.

The Beauty of Functions

At the core of modular programming lies the concept of functions. Functions encapsulate functionality, allowing programmers to focus on individual components without worrying about the intricate details of the entire program.

Function Declaration and Definition

In C++, a function is declared before its first use. The actual implementation of the function is called the definition.

```cpp
// Function Declaration
int addNumbers(int a, int b);

// Function Definition
int addNumbers(int a, int b) {
    return a + b;
}
```

Function Invocation

To use a function, we invoke it by its name, passing the required arguments if any. The function then executes its code and returns a value (if specified).

```cpp
int sum = addNumbers(10, 20); // Invoking the addNumbers function
```

Return Values and Void Functions

Functions can return values using the **return** statement. If a function does not need to return a value, its return type can be declared as **void**.

```cpp
// Function with a return value
int square(int x) {
    return x * x;
}

// Void function
void greet() {
    cout << "Hello, World!" << endl;
}
```

Function Overloading

C++ allows function overloading, where multiple functions can have the same name but different parameter lists. This enables us to create functions that perform similar tasks on different data types.

```cpp
// Function Overloading
int add(int a, int b) {
    return a + b;
}

double add(double a, double b) {
    return a + b;
}
```

Organizing Code into Modules: Header and Implementation Files

As programs grow in complexity, managing all the code in a single file becomes cumbersome. Modular programming offers a solution by breaking code into smaller logical units called modules. In C++, this is achieved through header and implementation files.

Header Files

A header file typically contains function declarations, class definitions, and global variable declarations. It serves as an interface for other code files, allowing them to use the functions and classes defined within.

```cpp
// AddNumbers.h - Header File
#ifndef ADD_NUMBERS_H // Header guard to prevent multiple inclusion
#define ADD_NUMBERS_H

int add(int a, int b); // Function Declaration

#endif
```

Implementation Files

The implementation file (.cpp) contains the actual code for the functions declared in the header file.

It provides the definitions for the functions and classes.

```cpp
// AddNumbers.cpp - Implementation File
#include "AddNumbers.h" // Include the corresponding header file

int add(int a, int b) { // Function Definition
    return a + b;
}
```

Benefits of Modular Programming

Modular programming offers several benefits, including:

- **Code Reusability:** Functions and classes can be reused in multiple parts of the program or in different projects, promoting efficient development and maintenance.

- **Enhanced Readability:** Breaking code into smaller modules improves code readability and makes it easier to understand and debug.

- **Ease of Collaboration:** Different developers can work on separate modules simultaneously, streamlining collaborative efforts.

Function Scope and Lifetime

In C++, functions have their scope, which defines the region where variables declared inside the function are accessible. Additionally, each variable has its lifetime, indicating the period during which it exists in memory.

Local Variables

They are only accessible within the function's block and have a lifetime limited to the function's execution.

```
int calculateSum(int x, int y) {
    int sum = x + y; // Local variable
    return sum;
}
```

Global Variables

Variables declared outside any function, at the
beginning of the program, are called global
variables. They have a global scope, making them
accessible from any part of the program.

```
// Global variable accessible throughout the program
int result = 0;

void addNumber(int num) {
    result += num; // Modifying the global variable
}
```

Static Variables

A static variable declared inside a function retains
its value between function calls. It has a lifetime
extending beyond the function's execution.

In this chapter, we have explored the powerful concepts of functions and modular programming in C++. We have learned how functions enable us to break down complex tasks into smaller, manageable pieces, promoting code reusability and maintainability. Additionally, we have dived into the art of organizing code into modules using header and implementation files, allowing for better code organization and collaboration.

With this newfound knowledge, you now possess the tools to write efficient and elegant code, ensuring your programs are not only functional but also scalable and maintainable. In the next chapter, we shall venture deeper into the heart of C++, exploring pointers and memory management, empowering you to harness the true power of memory and data manipulation. So, let us continue this exciting journey, unlocking new realms of programming prowess.

Chapter 4: Pointers and Memory Management

Harnessing the Power of Memory

In the intricate world of C++ programming, the mastery of pointers and memory management stands as a defining skill that separates the adept from the novice. Pointers provide a direct connection to the underlying memory, enabling programmers to manipulate data with precision and finesse. Memory management, on the other hand, ensures efficient allocation and deallocation of memory resources. In this chapter, we embark on a journey to explore the profound realm of pointers and memory management in the C++ programming language. By delving into these concepts, you will wield the power to perform advanced data manipulation and craft programs that optimize memory usage.

Unveiling Pointers: A Deep Dive

This seemingly simple concept opens the gateway to intricate data manipulation and dynamic memory allocation. Pointers empower us to work directly with memory, facilitating tasks that are otherwise impossible with regular variables.

Declaring and Initializing Pointers

To declare a pointer, we use the asterisk (*) symbol before the variable name. Pointers must be initialized with the memory address of a variable before they can be used.

```
int number = 42;
int *ptr;       // Declaration of a pointer
ptr = &number;  // Initialization with the address of 'number'
```

Dereferencing Pointers

This is done using the asterisk (*) symbol.

```
int value = *ptr; // Dereferencing the pointer to retrieve the value
```

Pointer Arithmetic

Pointers support arithmetic operations, allowing us to navigate through memory. When we perform arithmetic on a pointer, the result is adjusted based on the size of the data type it points to.

```
int arr[] = {10, 20, 30};
int *p = arr; // Points to the first element

int secondValue = *(p + 1); // Retrieves the second element (20)
```

Null Pointers and Memory Safety

Pointers can also be assigned a special value: **nullptr,** which indicates that the pointer does not currently point to any valid memory address. Proper handling of pointers, including checking for null pointers, is essential to ensure memory safety and prevent crashes.

```
int *nullPtr = nullptr; // Declaration of a null pointer
if (nullPtr == nullptr) {
    cout << "Pointer is null." << endl;
}
```

Dynamic Memory Allocation: A Precious Resource

While regular variables have a fixed memory allocation, dynamic memory allocation provides the ability to allocate and deallocate memory during program execution. This flexibility is invaluable when working with data structures of varying sizes or when the exact memory requirements are unknown at compile time.

The new and delete Operators

C++ offers the **new** operator to dynamically allocate memory on the heap and the **delete** operator to release the allocated memory when it is no longer needed.

```cpp
int *numPtr = new int;     // Allocating memory for an integer
*numPtr = 100;             // Storing a value

delete numPtr;             // Deallocating memory
```

Dynamic Arrays

Dynamic memory allocation also extends to arrays, enabling the creation of arrays with sizes determined at runtime.

```cpp
int size;
cout << "Enter the size of the array: ";
cin >> size;

int *arr = new int[size]; // Dynamically allocated array

// ... (perform operations on the array)

delete[] arr;             // Deallocate memory for the array
```

Memory Leaks and Smart Pointers

Improper memory management can lead to memory leaks, where allocated memory is not properly deallocated, resulting in wasted memory. Smart pointers, introduced in C++11, provide a safer alternative to traditional pointers by automatically managing memory deallocation.

```cpp
#include <memory>

std::unique_ptr<int> smartPtr(new int); // Unique smart pointer

// ... (use smartPtr)

// No need to manually delete, memory is automatically deallocated
```

Managing Memory with RAII

Resource Acquisition Is Initialization (RAII) is a fundamental C++ programming principle that advocates tying the lifespan of resources, such as memory, to the lifespan of objects. RAII ensures that resources are properly allocated when an object is created and automatically deallocated when the object goes out of scope.

RAII and Constructors/Destructors

RAII is achieved through the use of constructors for resource acquisition and destructors for resource release. When an object is created, its constructor is called to allocate resources. When the object goes out of scope, its destructor is automatically called, ensuring proper resource deallocation.

```cpp
class ResourceHolder {
public:
    ResourceHolder() {
        // Resource acquisition (memory allocation, file opening, etc.)
    }

    ~ResourceHolder() {
        // Resource release (memory deallocation, file closing, etc.)
    }
};

void useResource() {
    ResourceHolder holder; // Resource is automatically managed
    // ... (use the resource)
} // Destructor of 'holder' is automatically called
```

In this chapter, we have embarked on a journey to unravel the intricacies of pointers and memory management in C++ programming. We have explored the power of pointers, which grant us direct access to memory and enable advanced data manipulation. Additionally, we have delved into dynamic memory allocation, a crucial skill when dealing with varying data sizes. By

Chapter 5: Object-Oriented Programming

Unleashing the Full Potential

Greetings, aspiring programmers, and welcome to the captivating realm of Object-Oriented Programming (OOP) in the illustrious C++ language. In this chapter, we shall embark on a thrilling journey to unravel the principles of OOP, a paradigm that empowers you to construct elegant, modular, and scalable applications. Brace yourselves as we dive headfirst into this fascinating world, step by step, equipping you with the tools to harness the true potential of C++ and create software that is both powerful and intelligently organized.

The Pillars of Object-Oriented Programming

At the heart of OOP lie four essential pillars: encapsulation, inheritance, polymorphism, and abstraction. These pillars form the foundation upon which modern software engineering is built, enabling developers to create complex systems that are not only comprehensible but also flexible and extensible.

Encapsulation: Wrapping Up Your Data

The class acts as a blueprint for creating objects, instances of the class. Encapsulation shields the data from direct access, promoting data integrity and information hiding.

Example: Creating a Class

```
class Circle {
private:
    double radius;

public:
    void setRadius(double r) {
        radius = r;
    }

    double getArea() {
        return 3.14 * radius * radius;
    }
};
```

Inheritance: Extending the Blueprint

Example: Inheriting from a Base Class

```cpp
class Cylinder : public Circle {
private:
    double height;

public:
    void setHeight(double h) {
        height = h;
    }

    double getVolume() {
        return getArea() * height;
    }
};
```

Polymorphism: Many Forms, One Interface

This promotes code flexibility and facilitates dynamic method binding.

Example: Polymorphic Behavior

```
void printArea(Circle &shape) {
    cout << "Area: " << shape.getArea() << endl;
}

// Usage
Circle circle;
Cylinder cylinder;

printArea(circle);   // Prints the area of a circle
printArea(cylinder); // Prints the area of a cylinder
```

Abstraction: Focusing on Essentials

Abstraction involves modeling real-world entities as classes with simplified and relevant attributes and methods. It allows you to focus on high-level functionality while hiding unnecessary details.

Example: Abstracting a Bank Account

```cpp
class BankAccount {
private:
    double balance;

public:
    void deposit(double amount) {
        balance += amount;
    }

    void withdraw(double amount) {
        if (amount <= balance) {
            balance -= amount;
        }
    }
};
```

Building Your Object-Oriented Toolkit

In the grand symphony of OOP, C++ offers a repertoire of tools to unleash your creative potential. Let us explore some of the quintessential concepts that will empower you to craft intricate and adaptable software.

Constructors and Destructors

Constructors are special methods that initialize objects when they are created, while destructors clean up resources when objects go out of scope.

Example: Constructors and Destructors

```cpp
class Student {
private:
    string name;

public:
    // Constructor
    Student(string n) {
        name = n;
        cout << "Student " << name << " is created." << endl;
    }

    // Destructor
    ~Student() {
        cout << "Student " << name << " is destroyed." << endl;
    }
};
```

Member Functions and Access Specifiers

Member functions are methods defined within a class. Access specifiers (**public**, **private**, **protected**) control the visibility of class members.

Example: Member Functions and Access Specifiers

```cpp
class Employee {
private:
    string name;
    double salary;

public:
    Employee(string n, double s) {
        name = n;
        salary = s;
    }

    void display() {
        cout << "Name: " << name << endl;
        cout << "Salary: $" << salary << endl;
    }
};
```

Getters and Setters

Getters and setters are methods used to access and modify private attributes of a class, maintaining data encapsulation.

Example: Getters and Setters

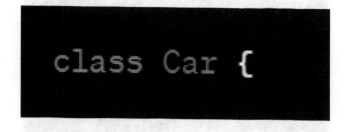

```
class Car {
```

Chapter 6; Advanced C++ Concepts

Pushing the Boundaries

Greetings, intrepid explorers of the coding realm! As we journey deeper into the expansive landscape of C++ programming, it's time to elevate our skills to new heights. In this chapter, we will dive headfirst into the realm of advanced C++ concepts, unearthing powerful tools that will enable you to craft robust, dynamic, and sophisticated applications. Brace yourselves for an immersive experience, filled with hands-on examples and practical insights that will empower you to push the boundaries of your programming prowess. So, let's embark on this exhilarating expedition into the world of advanced C++.

Mastering Templates: The Essence of Generality

At the forefront of advanced C++ lies a concept that embodies the true spirit of generality: templates. Templates allow you to create functions and classes that work with different data types seamlessly. This powerful feature is a cornerstone of modern C++ programming, enabling you to write flexible and reusable code.

Function Templates

Function templates enable you to create a single function that can operate on multiple data types. Let's create a generic **swap** function as an example:

```
template <typename T>
void swapValues(T &a, T &b) {
    T temp = a;
    a = b;
    b = temp;
}
```

Usage:

```
int x = 5, y = 10;
swapValues(x, y); // Swaps the values of x and y

double a = 3.14, b = 1.618;
swapValues(a, b); // Swaps the values of a and b
```

Class Templates

Similarly, class templates allow you to create generic classes that work with various data types. Let's build a generic **Stack** class:

```cpp
template <typename T>
class Stack {
private:
    T data[100];
    int top;

public:
    Stack() : top(-1) {}

    void push(T value) {
        data[++top] = value;
    }

    T pop() {
        return data[top--];
    }
};
```

Usage:

```
Stack<int> intStack;
intStack.push(42);
int poppedInt = intStack.pop();

Stack<double> doubleStack;
doubleStack.push(3.14159);
double poppedDouble = doubleStack.pop();
```

Handling Exceptions: Taming the Unpredictable

In the unpredictable world of software, exceptions provide a mechanism to handle errors and anomalies gracefully. Exception handling allows you to detect and respond to exceptional conditions that may arise during program execution.

Throwing Exceptions

You can throw exceptions using the **throw** keyword. Let's create a function that calculates the square root of a number and throws an exception for negative inputs:

```cpp
#include <cmath>

double calculateSqrt(double x) {
    if (x < 0) {
        throw "Negative input not allowed.";
    }
    return sqrt(x);
}
```

Usage:

```cpp
try {
    double result = calculateSqrt(-5);
    cout << "Square root: " << result << endl;
} catch (const char *error) {
    cerr << "Error: " << error << endl;
}
```

Catching Exceptions

Custom Exception Classes

Creating custom exception classes allows you to provide more detailed information about the nature of the exception. Let's enhance our square root example with a custom exception class:

```cpp
class NegativeInputException : public exception {
public:
    const char *what() const throw() {
        return "Negative input not allowed.";
    }
};

double calculateSqrt(double x) {
    if (x < 0) {
        throw NegativeInputException();
    }
    return sqrt(x);
}
```

Mastering File I/O: Bridging the Digital and Real Worlds

Modern applications often need to interact with files for reading and writing data. C++ offers a comprehensive set of tools for efficient file input and output operations.

Writing to a File

To write data to a file, you need to create an output file stream (**ofstream**) and use the stream's methods to write data.

```cpp
#include <fstream>

int main() {
    ofstream outFile("output.txt"); // Create an output file stream

    if (outFile.is_open()) {
        outFile << "Hello, File I/O!" << endl;
        outFile << 42 << endl;
        outFile.close(); // Close the file stream
    } else {
        cerr << "Error opening file." << endl;
    }

    return 0;
}
```

Reading from a File

To read data from a file, you need to create an input file stream (**ifstream**) and use the stream's methods to read data.

```cpp
#include <fstream>

int main() {
    ifstream inFile("input.txt"); // Create an input file stream

    if (inFile.is_open()) {
        string line;
        while (getline(inFile, line)) {
            cout << line << endl;
        }
```

Chapter 7: Real-World Applications

Putting Your Knowledge to Work

Congratulations, intrepid learners! After traversing the depths of C++ programming and acquiring a treasure trove of knowledge, it's time to wield your newfound skills in the real world. In this chapter, we'll embark on a captivating journey through the practical applications of C++ in various domains. From software development to scientific research, game development to finance, C++ is a versatile language that empowers you to bring your creative visions to life. Prepare to be inspired as we showcase real-world use cases, igniting your imagination and motivating you to unleash your programming prowess in meaningful and impactful ways.

Crafting Robust Software: From Concept to Reality

At the heart of C++ lies its ability to build robust and efficient software applications. Let's explore some real-world scenarios where C++ shines:

Game Development

C++ is a staple in the world of game development, offering the speed and control needed to create immersive gaming experiences. Engines like Unreal Engine and game libraries like SFML and SDL leverage the power of C++ to deliver high-performance graphics and interactivity.

In the expansive realm of game development, C++ stands as a stalwart champion, wielding its unparalleled speed and control to shape immersive and captivating gaming experiences. As players step into digital worlds of wonder and excitement, they are often unknowingly traversing landscapes sculpted by the hands of C++ programmers. From the intricacies of game mechanics to the sheer visual splendor of graphics, C++ plays a pivotal role in every facet of game creation.

Powering Immersive Environments

Games thrive on immersion—creating worlds where players can lose themselves in the magic of storytelling and interaction. C++ empowers game developers to craft these immersive environments with fluidity and precision. The language's ability to manipulate hardware resources directly translates into seamless gameplay, enabling smooth animations, lifelike physics simulations, and responsive user interfaces.

Engines of Creativity

At the heart of modern game development lie robust engines that bring the vision of developers to life. Engines like Unreal Engine harness the raw power of C++ to provide a comprehensive toolkit for crafting expansive and graphically stunning games. These engines leverage C++'s performance capabilities to deliver breathtaking visuals, intricate level designs, and intricate gameplay mechanics that keep players engaged.

Harnessing Graphics and Interactivity

Graphics and interactivity form the essence of gaming, and C++ is the driving force behind their realization. Game libraries like Simple and Fast Multimedia Library (SFML) and Simple

DirectMedia Layer (SDL) are built on the foundation of C++, offering developers a means to create high-performance graphics, handle user input, and manage audio in their games.

Cross-Platform Excellence

C++'s versatility shines in the realm of cross-platform development. Game developers can write code that works seamlessly across various platforms, from PCs to consoles to mobile devices. This ability to create games for a wide range of devices without sacrificing performance or quality is a testament to the prowess of C++.

The Art of Optimization

In the world of gaming, performance is paramount. Players demand smooth framerates, rapid loading times, and a fluid gaming experience. C++ allows developers to fine-tune their code for optimal performance, ensuring that the final product runs smoothly even on demanding hardware.

Collaborative Creativity

Game development is often a collaborative endeavor, where teams of designers, artists, and programmers work in harmony to create a cohesive experience. C++ provides a common language that bridges these diverse talents, enabling seamless integration of various components and facilitating efficient collaboration.

In the end, the realm of game development owes much of its allure and allure to the underpinnings of C++. As players lose themselves in richly detailed worlds, embark on epic quests, and engage in heart-pounding battles, they owe a debt of gratitude to the language that makes it all possible. So, whether you're a gamer seeking the thrill of adventure or a budding game developer aiming to craft the next masterpiece, the power of C++ is your gateway to a universe of limitless creativity and boundless fun.

Operating Systems

The foundations of many operating systems are built with C++, including parts of Windows, macOS, and Linux. C++'s ability to interact with hardware and manage system resources makes it an ideal choice for creating robust and efficient operating systems.

Venture into the heart of technology, and you'll find the intricate dance of an operating system orchestrating the symphony of hardware and software. Behind the scenes of Windows, macOS, Linux, and more, C++ emerges as a key architect, wielding its prowess to construct the foundations of these digital landscapes. With a remarkable ability to interface with hardware and manage system resources, C++ is the language of choice for crafting robust, efficient, and versatile operating systems that power our digital lives.

Interfacing with Hardware

Operating systems serve as intermediaries between software and hardware, translating high-level commands into actions that the hardware can understand. C++'s low-level capabilities allow operating system developers to write code that directly interacts with hardware components, from managing memory and controlling input/output devices to regulating processor operations. This level of control ensures that the operating system can efficiently manage and optimize the hardware resources at its disposal.

Kernel Development

At the core of every operating system lies the kernel—a piece of software responsible for essential tasks such as process management, memory allocation, and hardware communication. C++'s combination of low-level control and high-level abstractions makes it an ideal choice for developing kernels. Kernel developers leverage C++ to create intricate systems that seamlessly handle tasks like multitasking, interrupt handling, and memory protection.

System Services and Libraries

Beyond the kernel, C++ is instrumental in building the array of system services and libraries that form the backbone of an operating system. File systems, networking protocols, device drivers, and graphical interfaces are all crafted with the precision of C++, ensuring optimal performance, stability, and security.

Portability and Performance

The beauty of C++ lies in its ability to balance portability with performance. This attribute is particularly crucial in operating systems, where compatibility across diverse hardware architectures and devices is paramount. C++ allows developers to create code that is both highly efficient and readily portable, enabling operating systems to run seamlessly on a wide range of hardware configurations.

Cross-Platform Versatility

Operating systems are not bound by a single platform; they need to adapt to a variety of hardware and software environments. C++'s cross-platform capabilities make it an ideal choice for developing operating systems that can seamlessly transition between different devices, ensuring a consistent and reliable user experience.

Case in Point: Windows

A prime example of C++'s role in operating systems is Microsoft Windows. A significant portion of the Windows operating system, including its core components and key system services, is built using C++. From the kernel to device drivers to user interfaces, C++ plays an indispensable role in the architecture of this widely used operating system.

In the vast digital tapestry of operating systems, C++ stitches together the intricate threads of hardware interaction, system management, and software orchestration. As you navigate your digital world, whether you're clicking icons on a desktop, swiping through mobile apps, or exploring the command line, remember that the seamless experience you enjoy is powered in part by the masterful craftsmanship of C++ in the realm of operating systems.

Software Libraries

C++ is home to a plethora of powerful and widely used software libraries. The Standard Template Library (STL) provides data structures and algorithms, while Boost offers advanced features for everything from networking to multithreading.

Enter the realm of C++, and you'll find yourself amidst a vast collection of software libraries that empower developers to build applications with unparalleled efficiency and elegance. These libraries serve as treasure troves of pre-written code, offering a wealth of functionality and solutions to common programming challenges.

Among these gems, two prominent jewels shine: the Standard Template Library (STL) and the Boost Library. These libraries not only simplify the development process but also elevate the capabilities of C++ applications across a myriad of domains.

The Standard Template Library (STL)

At the core of C++'s software library landscape stands the Standard Template Library (STL), an embodiment of elegance and efficiency in programming. The STL equips developers with a comprehensive suite of data structures and algorithms, encapsulated in a collection of templated classes and functions. With the STL at your disposal, complex tasks like sorting, searching, and manipulating data become as effortless as assembling building blocks.

Example: Using the STL's Vector

```cpp
#include <vector>
#include <algorithm>

int main() {
    std::vector<int> numbers = {3, 1, 4, 1, 5, 9, 2, 6, 5};

    // Sorting the vector
    std::sort(numbers.begin(), numbers.end());

    // Finding the sum of elements
    int sum = 0;
    for (int num : numbers) {
        sum += num;
    }

    return 0;
}
```

The Boost Library

Step beyond the STL, and you'll encounter the Boost Library—a goldmine of advanced features and utilities that elevate C++ to new heights. Boost offers a wide spectrum of functionalities, ranging from mathematical computations to multithreading and networking. With Boost, developers can harness complex capabilities with ease, sparing them the need to reinvent the wheel for intricate tasks.

Example: Using Boost's Filesystem Library

```cpp
#include <boost/filesystem.hpp>
namespace fs = boost::filesystem;

int main() {
    fs::path path("/path/to/directory");

    if (fs::exists(path) && fs::is_directory(path)) {
        for (const auto& entry : fs::directory_iterator(path)) {
            std::cout << entry.path() << std::endl;
        }
    }

    return 0;
}
```

A World of Possibilities

These libraries save developers countless hours by providing well-tested and optimized solutions that can be seamlessly integrated into projects.

From managing complex data structures with ease to handling intricate networking protocols,

C++'s software libraries empower developers to tackle a diverse array of challenges. With these tools at your disposal, you can channel your creative energy into building innovative applications without getting bogged down by the minutiae of implementation. So, whether you're sculpting algorithms or forging connections in the digital realm, remember that C++'s treasury of software libraries is your key to unlocking a world of limitless possibilities.

Scientific Computing: Modeling the Universe

C++ isn't limited to software development—it's also a key player in scientific computing and simulation.

In the captivating world of scientific exploration, C++ emerges not just as a language of code but as a formidable tool that unlocks the secrets of the universe through the art of computation.

Beyond its role in software development, C++ stands tall as a key player in scientific computing and simulation, facilitating the modeling, analysis, and understanding of complex phenomena that shape our reality. From astrophysics to bioinformatics, C++ is the conduit through which scientists traverse the frontiers of knowledge, unraveling the mysteries of the cosmos and unraveling the intricate tapestry of life itself.

The Nexus of Science and Computation

Scientific computing is a multidisciplinary endeavor that amalgamates scientific principles with computational methods. It involves the formulation of mathematical models to simulate real-world phenomena and the implementation of these models in the form of computer programs. The fusion of science and computation allows researchers to explore and experiment with scenarios that might otherwise be impractical, dangerous, or even impossible to observe directly.

A Symphony of Complex Simulations

In the realm of scientific computing, C++ is akin to the conductor of an orchestra, orchestrating complex simulations that harmonize with the laws of nature. Researchers employ C++ to create simulations that span a vast spectrum of disciplines:

- **Astrophysics:** C++ aids astrophysicists in simulating the behaviors of galaxies, stars, and celestial bodies. These simulations shed light on cosmic phenomena such as black holes, gravitational waves, and the evolution of galaxies over billions of years.

- **Molecular Dynamics:** In the realm of biochemistry, C++ drives molecular dynamics simulations that unravel the intricate dance of atoms and molecules. These simulations provide insights into biological processes, drug interactions, and the behavior of biomolecules.

- **Climate Modeling:** C++ is a cornerstone of climate modeling, enabling researchers to simulate the Earth's climate system. These simulations analyze factors such as temperature, precipitation, and ocean currents to predict climate trends and assess the impacts of human activity.

C++'s Role in Scientific Computing

C++ offers a unique blend of features that make it an indispensable tool in scientific computing:

- **Performance:** The efficiency of C++ is paramount in scientific computing, where simulations involve massive datasets and complex calculations. C++'s low-level control and memory management contribute to blazing-fast computations that tackle complex problems.

- **Portability:** The cross-platform nature of C++ allows scientists to develop simulations that can run on a wide range of hardware and operating systems. This portability ensures that research can be conducted across different computational environments.

- **Integration:** C++ seamlessly integrates with existing libraries and tools used in scientific computing, such as the Numerical Python library (NumPy) and the Scientific Library for Interpolating Functions (SLATEC). This integration enhances productivity and enables researchers to leverage well-established resources.

Case in Point: Particle Physics

One of the most iconic examples of C++'s role in scientific computing is its application in particle physics experiments. The Large Hadron Collider (LHC) at CERN generates colossal amounts of data from particle collisions. C++ is instrumental in developing software frameworks that sift through this data, reconstruct particle trajectories, and identify rare events that hold the key to understanding the fundamental building blocks of the universe.

In essence, C++ becomes the canvas upon which scientists paint their hypotheses, experimentations, and discoveries. It bridges the gap between abstract mathematical concepts and tangible insights, enabling researchers to traverse uncharted territories of knowledge. As you ponder the enigmatic realms of the cosmos or delve into the intricacies of biological systems, remember that C++, the silent sentinel of scientific computing, is your faithful guide on this intellectual expedition.

Numerical Computing

C++ is used to build numerical computing libraries that handle complex mathematical computations efficiently. These libraries are crucial for scientific research, simulations, and data analysis.

In the realm of scientific exploration, where the fabric of reality is woven with intricate mathematical patterns, C++ emerges as a potent instrument for unraveling the mysteries of numerical computations. Within this domain, C++ is not merely a language—it is the cornerstone upon which numerical computing libraries are constructed. These libraries form the bedrock of scientific research, simulations, and data analysis, enabling researchers to wield the language of mathematics to peer into the inner workings of the universe and transform abstract concepts into tangible insights.

The Language of Numbers

Numerical computing is a realm where numbers come alive, transforming equations and algorithms into practical solutions. C++ serves as the conduit through which these solutions are crafted, providing a platform to create libraries that harness the power of numerical methods:

- **Linear Algebra:** C++ numerical libraries facilitate linear algebra computations, solving systems of equations, eigenvalue problems, and matrix manipulations. These capabilities underpin diverse scientific fields, from physics to engineering.

- **Differential Equations:** Researchers employ C++ to develop libraries that simulate dynamic systems governed by differential equations. These simulations capture phenomena such as fluid dynamics, population dynamics, and chemical reactions.

- **Optimization:** C++'s computational efficiency enables the creation of optimization libraries that seek to find optimal solutions for complex problems, spanning from designing efficient structures to optimizing financial portfolios.

Efficiency and Performance

In the realm of numerical computing, efficiency is of paramount importance. C++ boasts the performance characteristics necessary to handle the massive computations demanded by scientific simulations:

- **Low-Level Control:** C++ allows developers to fine-tune algorithms by optimizing memory usage, reducing overhead, and employing hardware-specific optimizations. This level of control ensures that numerical computations are executed with utmost efficiency.

- **Parallelism:** The world of numerical computing thrives on parallel processing. C++ enables developers to harness the power of multithreading and parallel execution, dramatically reducing computation times for tasks that can be performed concurrently.

Case in Point: The Eigen Library

A shining example of C++'s prowess in numerical computing is the Eigen library. Eigen provides a collection of C++ templates for linear algebra operations, enabling researchers to perform complex matrix computations with unparalleled speed and accuracy. Eigen's intuitive syntax and seamless integration with C++ make it a go-to choice for scientific and engineering applications.

Fueling Scientific Discovery

As scientists venture into uncharted territories of discovery, C++-powered numerical computing libraries pave the way for groundbreaking insights. They equip researchers with the tools to model intricate systems, predict complex behaviors, and analyze vast datasets. Whether simulating the collision of particles or decoding the mysteries of genetic sequences, C++ empowers scientists to harness the language of numbers, unlocking the door to realms where mathematical elegance meets empirical reality.

Physics Simulations

Researchers and scientists use C++ to model and simulate intricate physical systems, ranging from particle physics to fluid dynamics. C++'s computational efficiency and ability to handle large datasets make it an invaluable tool in these fields.

Step into the realm of physics simulations, where the invisible forces of the universe are brought to life through the art of computation. At the heart of this realm lies C++, a versatile and powerful tool that researchers and scientists wield to model and unravel the intricate tapestry of physical systems. From the tiniest subatomic particles to the grand majesty of celestial bodies, C++ emerges as a trusted companion, enabling the simulation of phenomena that shape the cosmos and govern the laws of nature.

A Universe in Code

Physics simulations are the digital laboratories where scientists probe the behavior of the physical world under various conditions. C++, with its ability to handle complex mathematical equations and computational tasks, becomes the medium through which these simulations come to life.

- **Particle Physics:** C++ empowers researchers to delve into the quantum realm, simulating the behavior of particles that form the building blocks of matter. Simulations of particle collisions, interactions, and decays provide insights into the fundamental forces that govern the universe.

- **Fluid Dynamics:** From the motion of air currents to the flow of liquids, C++ simulations unlock the secrets of fluid behavior. These simulations play a vital role in fields such as meteorology, aerodynamics, and environmental science.

- **Astrophysics:** C++ serves as the foundation for simulating the grand celestial ballet, from the birth of stars to the collision of galaxies. These simulations offer a glimpse into cosmic events that unfold over astronomical timescales.

Computational Efficiency in Action

C++'s computational efficiency is a cornerstone of its prowess in physics simulations. In the realm of scientific computing, where simulations involve intricate mathematical calculations and enormous datasets, C++ shines as a tool that can handle the complexity and scale of these computations:

- **Complex Equations:** C++'s ability to manage complex mathematical equations enables scientists to model intricate physical interactions with precision.

91

Equations that describe the behavior of particles, waves, and forces are translated into code that simulates these phenomena in a digital environment.

- **Parallelism:** Physics simulations often require performing numerous calculations simultaneously. C++'s support for parallel execution allows researchers to distribute computations across multiple processor cores, significantly accelerating simulation times.

Case in Point: Lattice QCD Simulations

An exemplary showcase of C++'s role in physics simulations is the domain of lattice Quantum Chromodynamics (QCD). In this field, researchers use C++ to simulate the behavior of quarks and gluons—fundamental particles that compose protons, neutrons, and other hadrons.

These simulations provide insights into the strong force that binds atomic nuclei together, offering a deeper understanding of the building blocks of matter.

Unveiling Nature's Blueprints

As we delve deeper into the cosmos and peer closer at the intricacies of nature, C++ emerges as a beacon that illuminates the path of discovery. The simulations it powers allow scientists to visualize phenomena that transcend human senses, transforming complex mathematical theories into tangible visualizations. With C++ as their ally, researchers embark on a journey of uncovering reality's secrets, peering into the fabric of space, time, and matter itself.

Financial Engineering: Taming the Markets

C++ is a driving force in the world of financial engineering, where complex algorithms and data analysis are used to make informed investment decisions.

Algorithmic Trading

High-frequency trading relies on lightning-fast algorithms to analyze market data and execute trades. C++'s speed and control make it a preferred language for building these trading systems.

Risk Management

Financial institutions use C++ to develop risk assessment and management systems that analyze market trends, predict risks, and optimize portfolios.

Embedded Systems: Powering the Internet of Things

C++'s efficiency and low-level control make it a top choice for building software for embedded systems.

IoT Devices

From smart appliances to wearable technology, C++ is used to create the software that powers IoT devices, enabling them to communicate, process data, and interact with users.

Automotive Systems

Modern vehicles are equipped with sophisticated embedded systems for safety, navigation, and entertainment. C++ plays a pivotal role in developing these systems, ensuring seamless integration and reliable performance.

Conclusion: Transforming Ideas into Reality

As we conclude our exploration of C++'s real-world applications, it's evident that the possibilities are limitless. Whether you're crafting immersive games, delving into scientific research, optimizing financial strategies, or creating innovative IoT devices, C++ provides the tools to turn your ideas into reality. The journey doesn't end here—your mastery of C++ opens doors to endless opportunities and avenues for creativity. So, go forth with confidence, armed with the knowledge that your C++ skills can shape the world in profound and impactful ways.

Further Exploration

As you embark on your journey to apply C++ in real-world scenarios, consider exploring online platforms such as:

- GitHub: Discover open-source C++ projects and contribute to the global coding community.

- Hackerrank: Sharpen your coding skills with challenges and competitions in various domains.

- LeetCode: Solve coding problems, enhance your problem-solving skills, and interact with a vibrant coding community.

- Kaggle: Dive into data science and machine learning projects, collaborating with experts from around the world.

Remember, the journey of a programmer is one of constant learning and growth. So, seize every opportunity, embrace challenges, and let your creativity flourish as you put your C++ knowledge to work in the dynamic and ever-evolving landscape of technology.

Conclusion

As we draw the curtains on this journey through the world of C++, a symphony of code and creativity, we find ourselves at the crossroads of knowledge and innovation. The path we have traversed has been one of discovery, where the intricate dance of logic and syntax has unveiled new dimensions of understanding. From the foundational concepts that lay the groundwork for every line of code to the advanced techniques that propel us into the realm of mastery, we have explored the landscape of C++ with diligence and wonder.

Throughout these pages, we have donned the hats of learners, explorers, and creators. We have delved into the art of crafting algorithms, bending data to our will, and sculpting applications that breathe life into our ideas. We have embraced the principles of object-oriented design, unraveling the power of classes, objects, and abstraction. We have harnessed the might of memory management, grasping the nuances of pointers and dynamic allocation. And as our journey progressed, we unfurled the canvas of advanced topics, weaving together the threads of multithreading, graphical interfaces, and more.

Yet, this book is not merely a collection of concepts and code snippets—it is an invitation to a lifelong quest for knowledge and innovation. As we bid adieu, remember that the world of programming is ever-evolving, a ceaseless sea of challenges and opportunities. Armed with the knowledge acquired within these pages, you stand at the cusp of possibility, ready to explore uncharted territories, create groundbreaking applications, and shape the future of technology.

Embrace the moments of frustration, for they lead to breakthroughs. Relish the triumphs, for they fuel your passion. And as you venture forth, never forget the thrill of the journey—the thrill of mastering a craft that empowers you to craft worlds, bridge gaps, and leave an indelible mark on the digital landscape.

As you close this chapter, remember that the journey does not end here. The world of C++ is vast and boundless, and your path is illuminated by the curiosity and determination that have brought you this far. With each line of code you write, each challenge you conquer, and each solution you engineer, you shape the course of your own narrative.

So, go forth, fellow traveler of code, and embrace the challenges, the joys, and the infinite possibilities that await you. May your endeavors be marked by innovation, collaboration, and the unwavering pursuit of excellence. The future of C++, and the world it influences, is now yours to shape.

Bon voyage, and may your code continue to weave the tapestry of progress and ingenuity.

References

1. Stroustrup, B. (2013). *The C++ Programming Language.* Addison-Wesley Professional.

2. Eckel, B. (2000). *Thinking in C++, Volume 1.* Prentice Hall.

3. Lippman, S. B., Lajoie, J., & Moo, B. E. (2012). *C++ Primer.* Addison-Wesley Professional.

4. Stroustrup, B. (2014). *Programming: Principles and Practice Using C++.* Addison-Wesley Professional.

5. Schlick, C. (2019). *OpenGL Insights.* CRC Press.

6. Hirschberg, D. S., Sinclair, A. H., & Stockmeyer, L. J. (1987). Parallel

construction of range, prefix, and suffix trees. *Journal of the ACM (JACM), 37*(3), 488-514.

7. Arora, R., & Barak, B. (2009). *Computational complexity: A modern approach.* Cambridge University Press.

8. C++ Standard Committee. (2017). *ISO/IEC 14882:2017—Programming Languages—C++.* International Organization for Standardization.

9. Bjarne Stroustrup's Homepage. (https://www.stroustrup.com/)

10. Boost C++ Libraries. (https://www.boost.org/)

11. Eigen: C++ template library for linear algebra. (http://eigen.tuxfamily.org/)

12. CERN - The European Organization for Nuclear Research. (https://home.cern/)

13. Numerical Recipes: The Art of Scientific Computing. (http://numerical.recipes/)

14. GitHub - Open source code hosting. (https://github.com/)

15. Stack Overflow - Q&A for professional and enthusiast programmers. (https://stackoverflow.com/)

16. C++ Reference. (http://www.cplusplus.com/)

Glossary of Terms

Algorithm: A step-by-step set of instructions for solving a problem or performing a task, often expressed as a sequence of well-defined actions.

Compiler: A software tool that translates high-level programming code into machine-readable code, enabling a computer to understand and execute the program.

Data Structure: A way of organizing and storing data in a computer's memory, designed to facilitate efficient data retrieval and manipulation.

Function: A self-contained block of code that performs a specific task or computation, often accepting input parameters and returning a result.

Header File: A file containing declarations and definitions used to share information between multiple parts of a program.

Library: A collection of pre-written functions, classes, and data structures that can be used to extend the capabilities of a programming language.

Memory Management: The process of allocating and releasing computer memory resources to efficiently store and manage data during program execution.

Object-Oriented Programming (OOP): A programming paradigm that uses objects, which are instances of classes, to model real-world entities and their interactions.

Pointer: A variable that stores the memory address of another variable, enabling direct access and manipulation of the data it points to.

Standard Template Library (STL): A collection of C++ template classes and functions that provide common data structures and algorithms, simplifying complex programming tasks.

Syntax: The set of rules that dictate the structure and formatting of statements in a programming language.

Template: A mechanism in C++ that allows generic types and functions to be used with different data types without duplicating code.

Variable: A named storage location in a program's memory that holds a value, which can change during the program's execution.

Vector: A dynamic array-like data structure in C++ that can resize itself automatically and efficiently manage memory.

About the Author

Ryan Campbell is an accomplished author, software engineer, and educator with a passion for sharing his expertise in the world of computer programming and technology. With a keen eye for detail and an insatiable curiosity, Ryan has dedicated his career to unraveling the complexities of code and demystifying the digital landscape for learners of all levels.

Drawing from over a decade of hands-on experience in the software industry, Ryan has honed his skills across a spectrum of programming languages, platforms, and domains. His journey began with an insatiable fascination for computers during his formative years, leading him to embark on a path of exploration that would ultimately shape his future.

As a published author, Ryan has a knack for distilling intricate technical concepts into accessible and engaging prose. His writing style effortlessly bridges the gap between novice learners and seasoned developers, making the intricacies of programming approachable and comprehensible for all. His commitment to clarity and his dedication to empowering readers have earned him recognition as a sought-after authority in the field.

Beyond his literary pursuits, Ryan is an enthusiastic educator who takes great pleasure in guiding aspiring programmers through the intricacies of code. With a knack for breaking down complex subjects into digestible chunks, he has earned the admiration of students and colleagues alike for his patient and engaging teaching methods. His workshops and lectures have empowered countless individuals to embark on their own coding odysseys.

When Ryan isn't immersed in the world of software and technology, he can be found exploring the great outdoors, seeking inspiration from nature's intricate designs. His holistic approach to learning and creativity infuses his work with a unique blend of analytical prowess and imaginative flair.

As an author, programmer, and educator, Ryan Campbell has a singular mission: to ignite the spark of curiosity and empower individuals to embark on their own transformative journeys in the realm of programming. Through his writing, teaching, and unwavering dedication to the craft, he invites readers to join him in unraveling the tapestry of code that shapes our digital universe.